What's New in *The Internet Unleashed,* Second Edition

Expanded Coverage of the World Wide Web

In the last year, the use of the Web has exploded. With popular browsers such as Mosaic and Netscape, Web access has become as important as Internet access. Web information is integrated throughout the book, but for a primer, turn to Chapter 28, "Navigating the World Wide Web."

New Chapters

- **Chapter 1, "The Idea of the Internet."** Author Jill Ellsworth discusses how the Internet has affected society.
- **Chapter 19, "Internet Teleconferencing: MBone, CU-SeeMe, and Maven."** Kevin Mullet examines one of the hottest topics on the Internet: teleconferencing.
- **Chapter 30, "New Tools: FSP, Harvest, and Hyper-G."** Billy Barron presents three new tools available on the Internet and gives odds on whether they'll flourish in the coming years.
- **Chapter 33, "Providing Information with E-Mail Robots."** Dave Taylor considers two different e-mail auto-responders that offer simple ways to automate the way you respond to electronic mail.
- **Chapter 36, "Creating Web Pages with HTML."** Brandon Plewe provides an up-and-running tutorial on how to use HTML to create your own Web pages.
- **Chapter 37, "Setting Up a World Wide Web Server."** Kevin Mullet shows readers how to create their own Web sites.
- **Chapter 42, "Digital Cash."** Rosalind Resnick presents methods online merchants are using to handle the issue of legal tender and payments for goods and services.
- **Chapter 62, "How the Web Is Changing the Internet."** John December examines how the popularity of the World Wide Web and graphical browsers have changed—and are still changing—the way information is presented on the Internet.
- **Chapter 63, "Spamming and Cancelbots."** Kevin Savetz discusses the mass posting of a message to too many newsgroups (spamming) and programs written by annoyed Internetters to remove the offending message (cancelbots).
- **Chapter 66, "Games Online."** Kevin Savetz shows readers how to relax and have fun with the Internet by seeking out the best games.
- **Chapter 67, "Cool Web Worlds."** Angela Gunn takes readers on two tours of the best of the Web.
- **Chapter 68, "Online Art Galleries."** Angela Gunn presents the intersection of art and the Internet.

As a final note, everyone knows that the Internet is in a constant state of flux. As a result, in addition to these new chapters, many of the old chapters have new and updated information.